NOW
IS YOUR
TIME

Book design © Deseret Book Company

Cover image: may/Adobe Stock

Interior images: Tree illustration/gaga vastard/Adobe Stock,
    Mountain illustration/twelve.std/Adobe Stock

Art direction: Richard Erickson

Design: Kensie Smith

Library of Congress Cataloging-in-Publication Data

Names: Nelson, Russell M. (Russell Marion), 1924– author.

Title: Now is your time: a message to the rising generation / Russell M. Nelson.

Description: Salt Lake City, Utah: Deseret Book, [2023] | Includes bibliographical references. | Audience: Ages 11–18 | Audience: Grades 10–12 | Summary: "President Russell M. Nelson of The Church of Jesus Christ of Latter-day Saints pens a message to the rising generation of the Church"—Provided by publisher.

Identifiers: LCCN 2022061834 | ISBN 9781639931484 (hardback)

Subjects: LCSH: Latter-day Saint youth—Religious life. | Latter-day Saint youth—Conduct of life.

Classification: LCC BX8643. Y6 N45 2023 | DDC 248.8/3—dc23/eng/20230329

LC record available at https: //lccn.loc.gov/2022061834

Printed in the United States of America
Sun Print Solutions, Salt Lake City, UT

10   9   8   7   6   5   4   3   2

A MESSAGE TO THE

NOW
IS YOUR
TIME

RISING GENERATION

RUSSELL M. NELSON

DESERET
BOOK

On May 15, 1829, the Prophet Joseph Smith and Oliver Cowdery knelt in a secluded spot in the woods near Joseph and Emma's home in Harmony, Pennsylvania. Sister Nelson and I have been to that grove of sugar maples.

This grove became sacred when John the Baptist conferred the Aaronic Priesthood upon Joseph Smith and Oliver Cowdery.

Later, Peter, James, and John restored the Melchizedek Priesthood in the same general area.

In September 2015, I dedicated that Priesthood Restoration Site. **Of all the previous assignments I had then received, that was the most significant to me.** That site commemorates the restoration of priesthood authority and keys to man upon the earth. Those and other keys were needed to lead the restored Church of Jesus Christ and make it possible for us to perform and receive essential ordinances, including sealing families together for eternity. That day of dedication was a singular moment in my life!

Now, this is a singular time in *your* life. There won't be another quite like it. You are establishing priorities and patterns that will dramatically affect not just your mortal life but also your eternal life.

Let us talk about life. That is something with which I have had a little experience. I grew up during a Great Depression. I was a teenager during World War II. I have had several brushes with death. I have been to six continents many times and have yet to meet a people or culture that I did not find inspiring.

I have also borne grief. I have watched two precious daughters be slowly, painfully, and fatally consumed by cancer. And I have buried a magnificent wife, Dantzel, the mother of our 10 children. Knowing that it is not good for man to be alone,[1] I chose to marry again. I married another remarkable woman, dear Wendy.

This is a singular time in your life. There won't be another quite like it.

You are establishing priorities and patterns that will dramatically affect not just your mortal life but also your eternal life.

I have seen friends and family members make heroic choices and live exemplary lives. And I have seen others make disastrous decisions that have derailed their potential.

In short, I have lived a long time, and at this point, I have stopped buying green bananas! And I have also stopped spending time on things that don't matter. But *you* do matter to me! And your future matters much to me!

> I have also stopped spending time on things that don't matter. But *you* do matter to me! And your future matters much to me!

Sister Nelson and I recently attended the inauguration of a university president. During that excellent event, I thought about the countless educators worldwide who are dedicated to teaching men and women your age. **Education is very important. I consider it a religious responsibility. The glory of God is intelligence.**[2]

There is a major difference, however, between the responsibilities of secular educators and my responsibility as the senior Apostle on earth. Their job is to educate and prepare you for your *mortal* experience—meaning, how to succeed in your life's work. My responsibility is to educate and prepare

*Education is
very important.
I consider it
a religious
responsibility.*

*The glory of God
is intelligence.*

you also for your *immortal* experience—meaning, how to gain eternal life.

Teachings of the finest institutions of higher learning have limitations, because secular education generally ignores three major truths that are rarely addressed:

- First, each of us is going to die.[3]
- Second, because of Jesus Christ, each of us is going to be resurrected and become immortal.[4]
- And third, Judgment Day is ahead for each of us.[5]

These three absolute truths should form the foundation of your spiritual education.

Because of the Restoration of the gospel of Jesus Christ in its fulness, we know a lot about our post-mortal possibilities. We know that our Father's house has many mansions.[6] We know that God loves His children so much that, as President Dallin H. Oaks has taught, "*all the children of God*"—with the fewest of exceptions—will "wind up in a kingdom of *glory*."[7] Just think of

> Our Father created kingdoms of *glory*—telestial, terrestrial, and celestial— to provide a glorious place for His children.

8

it! Our Father created kingdoms of *glory*—telestial, terrestrial, and celestial—to provide a glorious place for His children.

My purpose is to make sure that your eyes are wide open to the truth that this life really *is* the time when you get to decide what kind of life *you* want to live forever. Now *is* your time "to prepare to meet God."[8]

Mortal lifetime is hardly a nanosecond compared with eternity. But, my dear brothers and sisters, what a crucial nanosecond it is! During this life we get to choose which laws we are willing to obey—those of the celestial kingdom, or the terrestrial, or the telestial[9]—and, therefore, in which kingdom of glory we will live forever.

> **Mortal lifetime is hardly a nanosecond compared with eternity.**

Every righteous choice that you make here will pay huge dividends now. But **righteous choices in mortality will pay unimaginable dividends eternally.** If you choose to make covenants with God and are faithful to those covenants, you have the promise of "glory added upon [your head] for ever and ever."[10]

These truths ought to prompt your ultimate sense of FOMO—or fear of missing out. You have

This life really *is* the time when you get to decide what kind of life *you* want to live forever.

Now *is*
your time "to
prepare to
meet God."

*Righteous choices
in mortality
will pay
unimaginable
dividends
eternally.*

the potential to reach the celestial kingdom. The ultimate FOMO would be missing out on the celestial kingdom, settling for a lesser kingdom because here on earth you chose only to live the laws of a lesser kingdom.

The adversary, of course, does not want you even to think about tomorrow, let alone eternal life. But please don't be uninformed or naive about the opportunities and challenges of mortality. In that spirit, you need to understand three fundamental truths that will help you prepare your future course:

- First, know the truth about who you are.
- Second, know the truth about what Heavenly Father and His Son have offered you.
- And third, know the truth related to your conversion.

I will speak to each of these three points.

First: Know the truth about who you are.

I believe that if the Lord were speaking to you directly, the first thing He would make sure you understand is your true identity.[11] My dear friends, you are literally spirit children of God. You have

*The way you
think about who
you really are*

*affects almost
every decision
you will
ever make.*

sung this truth since you learned the words to "I Am a Child of God."[12] But is that eternal truth imprinted upon your heart? Has this truth rescued you when confronted with temptation?[13]

I fear that you may have heard this truth so often that it sounds more like a slogan than divine truth. And yet, **the way you think about who you really are affects almost every decision you will ever make.**

In 2006, when I married Wendy, I was in for several surprises—most of them quite wonderful. One of those surprises was the number of clothing items she owned that displayed a logo—universities from which she graduated, places she had traveled, and so forth. Whenever she wore one of those items, I teased her by saying, "Who are you advertising today?" She invited me to join in the fun!

Labels *can* be fun and indicate your support for any number of positive things. Many labels will change for you with the passage of time. And not all labels are of equal value. But **if any label replaces your most important identifiers, the results can be spiritually suffocating.**

For example, if I were to rank in order of importance the designations that could be applied to me, I

If any label replaces your most important identifiers, the results can be spiritually suffocating.

Who are you?

First and foremost, you are a child of God.

would say: First, I am a child of God—a son of God—then a son of the covenant, then a disciple of Jesus Christ and a devoted member of His restored Church.

Next would come my honored titles as a husband and father, then Apostle of the Lord Jesus Christ.

All other labels that have applied to me—such as a medical doctor, surgeon, researcher, professor, lieutenant, captain, PhD, American, and so forth—would fall somewhere down the list.

Now, let us turn the question to you. *Who are you?*

First and foremost, you are a child of God.

Second, as a member of the Church, you are a child of the covenant. And third, you are a disciple of Jesus Christ.

I plead with you not to *replace* these three paramount and unchanging identifiers with any others, because doing so could stymie your progress or pigeonhole you in a stereotype that could potentially thwart your eternal progression.

For example, if you are identified mainly as an American, those who are not Americans may think, "I know everything there is to know about you" and attribute erroneous beliefs to you.

If you identify yourself by your political affiliation, you will instantly be categorized as having certain beliefs—though I don't know anyone who believes everything that their preferred political party presently embraces.

We could go on and on, rehearsing the constraints of various labels that we put on ourselves or that other people place upon us.

> Ageism, racism, nationalism, sexism, and a host of other "isms" are universally limiting.

Some might label me as an "old man." But I'm a lot younger than Adam was—and Noah too.[14] Ageism, racism, nationalism, sexism, and a host of other "isms" are universally limiting.

How tragic it is when someone believes the label another person has given them. Imagine the heartache of a child who is told, "You are dumb." Identifiers and labels are powerful!

The adversary rejoices in labels because they divide us and restrict the way we think about ourselves and each other. How sad it is when we honor labels more than we honor each other.

Labels can lead to judging and animosity. **Any *abuse* or *prejudice* toward another because of** nationality, race, sexual orientation, gender, educational degrees, culture, or other significant identifiers is offensive to our Maker! Such mistreatment causes us to live beneath our stature as His covenant sons and daughters!

There are various labels that may be very important to you, of course. Please do not misunderstand me. I am not saying that other designations and identifiers are not significant. I am simply saying that no identifier should *displace*, *replace*, or *take priority over* these three enduring designations: "child of God," "child of the covenant," and "disciple of Jesus Christ."

Any identifier that is not compatible with these three basic designations will ultimately let you down. Other labels will disappoint you in time because they do not have the power to lead you toward eternal life in the celestial kingdom of God.

Worldly identifiers will *never* give you a vision of who you can ultimately become. They will never affirm your divine DNA or your unlimited, divine potential.

Because there is a grand plan of salvation authored by Heavenly Father, does it not stand to reason that you also have a divine destiny?[15]

Make no mistake
about it:
Your potential
is divine.

With your diligent seeking, God will give you glimpses of who you may become.

Make no mistake about it: Your potential is divine. With your diligent seeking, God will give you glimpses of who you may become.

So who are you? First and foremost, you are a child of God, a child of the covenant, and a disciple of Jesus Christ. As you embrace these truths, our Heavenly Father will help you reach your ultimate goal of living eternally in His holy presence.

> **First and foremost, you are a child of God, a child of the covenant, and a disciple of Jesus Christ.**

Second: Know the truth about what God the Father and His Son, Jesus Christ, have offered you.

In short, They have offered you everything!

Heavenly Father's plan for His children allows us to live where and how He lives and ultimately to become more and more like Him. His plan literally makes the richest blessings of all eternity available to us, including the potential for us to become "joint-heirs with Christ."[16]

God knows all and sees all. In all of eternity, no one will ever know you or care about you more than He does. No one will ever be closer to you than He is.

You can pour out your heart to Him and trust Him to send the Holy Ghost and angels to care for you. He demonstrated His ultimate love when He sent His Only Begotten Son to die for you—to be your Savior and your Redeemer!

Through His Atonement, the Lord Jesus Christ overcame the world.[17] Therefore, He is "mighty to . . . cleanse [you] from all unrighteousness."[18] He will deliver you from your most excruciating circumstances in His own way and time.[19] As you come unto Him in faith, He will guide, preserve, and protect you. He will heal your broken heart and comfort you in your distress.[20] He will give you access to His power. And He will make the impossible in your life become possible.

Jesus Christ is the only enduring source of hope, peace, and joy for you. Satan can never replicate any of these. And Satan will never help you.

On the other hand, God's work and His glory is to bring about the "immortality and eternal life of man."[21] God will do everything He can, short of violating your agency, to help you not miss out on the greatest blessings in all eternity.

God has a special love for each person who makes a covenant with Him in the waters of baptism.[22] And

Jesus Christ is the only enduring source

*of hope, peace,
and joy for you.*

that divine love deepens as additional covenants are made and faithfully kept. Then at the end of mortal life, precious is the reunion of each covenant child with our Heavenly Father.[23]

He also cares *deeply* that all His children have an opportunity to hear the glad tidings of the restored gospel. Heavenly Father has sent His children to earth for more than six millennia. Most of these people have not yet received the ordinances that would qualify them for eternal life. That is why temples are so significant. That is why the gathering of Israel on both sides of the veil is *the* most important cause on earth today. You, my dear colleagues in this holy work, have an essential role in this gathering, and I thank you for it.

This now leads me to my third point.

Know the truth related to your conversion.

The truth is that you must own your own conversion. No one else can do it for you.

Now, may I invite you to consider a few questions? Do you want to feel peace about concerns that presently plague you? Do you want to know Jesus

You must
own your own
conversion.
No one else can
do it for you.

Take charge of your testimony.

Work for it.
Own it.
Care for it.
Nurture it so
that it will grow.
Feed it truth.

Christ better? Do you want to learn how His divine power can heal your wounds and weaknesses? Do you want to experience the sweet, soothing power of the Atonement of Jesus Christ working in your life?

Seeking to answer these questions will require effort—much effort. I plead with you to take charge of your testimony. Work for it. Own it. Care for it. Nurture it so that it will grow. Feed it truth. Don't pollute it with the false philosophies of unbelieving men and women and then wonder why your testimony is waning.

Engage in daily, earnest, humble prayer. Nourish yourself in the words of ancient and modern prophets. Ask the Lord to teach you how to hear Him better. Spend more time in the temple and in family history work.

As you make your testimony your highest priority, watch for miracles to happen in your life.

If you have questions—and I hope you do—seek answers with the fervent desire to believe. Learn all you can about the gospel and be sure to turn to truth-filled sources for guidance. We live in the

As you make your testimony your highest priority, watch for miracles to happen in your life.

Your sincere questions, asked in faith,

will *always*
lead to greater
faith and more
knowledge.

dispensation when "nothing shall be withheld."[24] Thus, in time, the Lord will answer all our questions.

> **The Lord will answer all our questions.**

In the meantime, immerse yourself in the rich reservoir of revelation we have at our fingertips. I promise that doing so will strengthen your testimony, even if some of your questions are not yet answered. **Your sincere questions, asked in faith, will _always_ lead to greater faith and more knowledge.**

If friends and family should step away from the Church, continue to love them. It is not for you to judge another's choice any more than you deserve to be criticized for staying faithful.

Now, please hear me when I say: Do not be led astray by those whose doubts may be fueled by things _you cannot see_ in their lives. Most of all, let your skeptical friends see how much _you_ love the Lord and His gospel. Surprise their doubting hearts with your believing heart!

As you take charge of your testimony and cause it to grow, you will become a more potent instrument in the hands of the Lord. You will be "inspired by a better cause"[25]—the cause of Jesus Christ!

There is nothing happening on this earth more important than gathering Israel *for Him*. Let your Heavenly Father know that you want to help. Ask Him to put you to work in this glorious cause. And then stand back and marvel at what happens when you let God prevail in your life.

> There is nothing happening on this earth more important than gathering Israel *for Him*.

My dear young friends, I love you. I thank you. I believe in you. As the Lord's prophet, I bless you to know the truth about who you are and to treasure the truth about what your glorious potential really is. I bless you to take charge of your own testimony. And I bless you to have the desire and strength to keep your covenants.

As you do, I promise that you will experience spiritual growth, freedom from fear, and a confidence that you can scarcely imagine now. You will have the strength to have a positive influence far beyond your natural capacity. And I promise that your future will be more exhilarating than anything you can presently believe.

> Your future will be more exhilarating than anything you can presently believe.

You will experience spiritual growth, freedom from fear,

and a confidence that you can scarcely imagine now.

Notes

1. See Genesis 2:18; Moses 3:18; Abraham 5:14.
2. See Doctrine and Covenants 93:36.
3. See 1 Corinthians 15:22.
4. See John 11:25.
5. See Mormon 3:20.
6. See John 14:2; Joseph Smith Translation, 1 Corinthians 15:40 (in 1 Corinthians 15:40, footnote *a*); Doctrine and Covenants 76:89–98; 131:1.
7. Dallin H. Oaks, "Divine Love in the Father's Plan," *Liahona*, May 2022, 101.
8. See Alma 12:24; 34:32.
9. See Doctrine and Covenants 88:22–24.
10. Abraham 3:26.
11. This is what the Lord taught the people of ancient

America when He spoke to them. After identifying who *He* was, He told His listeners who *they* were: "And behold, *ye are the children of the prophets; and ye are of the house of Israel; and ye are of the covenant*" (3 Nephi 20:25; emphasis added). These exact truths were also declared to people in biblical times (see Acts 3:25).

12. "I Am a Child of God," *Hymns*, no. 301.

13. As young women and young men, you quote themes that begin "I am a beloved daughter of heavenly parents, with a divine nature and eternal destiny" and "I am a beloved son of God, and He has a work for me to do" (*General Handbook: Serving in The Church of Jesus Christ of Latter-day Saints*, 11.1.2, 10.1.2, ChurchofJesus Christ.org).

14. Adam died at age 930 (see Genesis 5:5); Noah died at age 950 (see Genesis 9:29).

15. President Orson Hyde (1805–78), President of the Quorum of the Twelve Apostles, said that "we understood things better [in the premortal world] than we do in this lower world." He continued, surmising about promises we likely made there: "It is not impossible that we signed the articles thereof with our own hands, which articles may be retained in the archives above, to be presented to us when we rise from the dead, and be judged out of our own mouths, according to that which is written in the books" ("Remarks," *Deseret News*, Dec. 21, 1859, 322).

16. Romans 8:17.
17. See John 16:33; Doctrine and Covenants 50:41.
18. Alma 7:14.
19. The Lord is mighty to deliver us just as He delivered Nephi from the clutches of Laban (see 1 Nephi 4:3).
20. See Luke 4:18; Alma 7:10–12.
21. Moses 1:39.
22. In the Hebrew language of the Old Testament, the word for God's covenant love is *hesed*.
23. See Psalm 116:15.
24. Doctrine and Covenants 121:28.
25. Alma 43:45: "For they were not fighting for monarchy nor power but they were fighting for their homes and their liberties, their wives and their children, and their all, yea, for their rites of worship and their church."

Notes

Notes